After early experience J. C. Williamson's, Sydney University Dramatic Society (SUDS), Nimrod Theatre and Melbourne Theatre Company, Nick Enright trained for the theatre at New York University School of the Arts, where he studied playwriting with Israel Horovitz.

His plays include *On the Wallaby*, *Daylight Saving*, *St James Infirmary*, *Mongrels*, *A Property of the Clan*, *The Quartet from Rigoletto*, *Blackrock*, *Good Works*, *Playgrounds*, *Spurboard*, *Chasing the Dragon*, *A Man with Five Children* and *A Poor Student*. With Justin Monjo, he adapted Tim Winton's *Cloudstreet* for the stage.

For film Nick wrote *Lorenzo's Oil* with George Miller (for which they were nominated for Academy and WGA Awards for Best Original Screenplay), and *Blackrock*; and for television *Coral Island* and the miniseries *Come In Spinner*. Many of his plays have been broadcast and he also wrote original work for radio.

With composer Terence Clarke, he wrote the musicals *The Venetian Twins* and *Summer Rain*. Other musical collaborations include *Miracle City* with Max Lambert, *Mary Bryant* and *The Good Fight* with David King and the book for the Australian production of *The Boy From Oz*.

*Good Works* and *Cloudstreet* won Melbourne Green Room Awards for Best Play. *Daylight Saving*, *A Property of the Clan*, *Blackrock* (screenplay) and *Cloudstreet* have all won Writers' Guild Gold AWGIE Awards. Nick was honoured to receive the 1998 Sidney Myer Performing Arts Award.

Nick had long been involved as a teacher and writer with young actors, especially at the National Institute of Dramatic Art (NIDA) and the Western Australia Academy of Performing Arts (WAAPA), as well as community based companies such as Freewheels. He was instrumental in setting up, with Jessica Machin and Julian Louis, (State of) Play, an actor ensemble in Sydney which develops and presents new works.

Nick Enright died in Sydney in March 2003.

First published in 1990 by
Currency Press Pty Ltd
Gadigal Land, Suite 310, 46–56 Kippax Street, Surry Hills, NSW 2010, Australia
www.currency.com.au
enquiries@currency.com.au

Reprinted 2005, 2008, 2012, 2022

NATIONAL LIBRARY OF AUSTRALIA CIP DATA

    Enright, Nicholas, 1950–
    Daylight Saving
    ISBN 9780868192659
    I. Title.
    A822.3

Typeset by Emily Ralph for Currency Press
Cover design by Kate Florance for Currency Press

Currency Press acknowledges the Traditional Owners of the Country on which we live and work. We pay our respects to all Aboriginal and Torres Strait Islander Elders, past and present.

This publication has been assisted by the Commonwealth Government through the Australia Council, its arts funding and advisory body.

# Nick Enright
# Daylight Saving

**CURRENCY PRESS**
The performing arts publisher

*For Sandy, and for David, with thanks*

*Daylight Saving* was first produced by the Ensemble Theatre, Sydney on 21 September 1989 with the following cast:

| | |
|---|---|
| TOM | Neil Fitzpatrick |
| FLICK | Sandy Gore |
| BUNTY | Diana Davidson |
| JOSH | Barry Langrish |
| STEPHANIE | Linden Wilkinson |
| JASON | Alex Morcos |

Directed by Peter Kingston
Designed by Monita Roughsedge

AUTHOR'S NOTE

*Daylight Saving* was given a rehearsed reading by the Sydney Theatre Company at The Wharf on 6 June 1988 under the direction of George Ogilvie. My thanks to George and the actors and to the STC for offering valuable help in bringing the play to its present form. Informal workshop facilities were graciously provided by the management of The Glendale, though I brought the scones. Hilary Linstead, Viccy Harper and their tireless cohorts have my undying gratitude. Thanks, finally, to Sandra Bates and the Ensemble Theatre for producing the play, and to Peter Kingston and his splendid cast and production team, named above; and to my friends, whose encouragement and support have meant more than they know.

CHARACTERS

> TOM FINN, forty-two
> FELICITY (FLICK), TOM's wife, thirty-seven
> BUNTY, FLICK's mother
> JOSHUA MAKEPEACE, thirty-seven
> STEPHANIE
> JASON STRUTT, twenty-one

SETTING

The play is set in a house overlooking Pittwater, north of Sydney. The action takes place on two consecutive Saturdays in March, the second of which is the night daylight saving ends and the clocks are put back an hour.

# ACT ONE

## SCENE ONE

*The living-room and deck of* FLICK *and* TOM's *house. The front door is prominent. There are two other doors - a swinging door to the kitchen, and a door or hallway to bedrooms and bathroom. The house next door is accessible from one end of the deck. The room is casually but elegantly furnished – a rug over polished wood floors, sofas, dining table and chairs, a TV and VCR, books, pictures and photographs on the walls. Beyond the windows and past the deck, there is an impression of height, of trees. The deck has a view of Pittwater. The house is high, the front door a fair climb up steps from the road.* FLICK *is at the front door, waving off an unseen group, who are calling goodbyes and thank-yous.*

FLICK: My pleasure.

> *She closes the door.*

My pleasure? I've had more fun at the dentist's.

> *She examines a spot in the rug.*

Burnt right through. Thanks, guys.

> *A key turns in the front door.* TOM *hurries in, casually dressed, carrying a briefcase.*

TOM: That's quite a crew.

FLICK: You're not kidding. The sound guy put out his cigarette on the rug.

TOM: You got off lightly. I'm running, Flix. Can you pack those files for me?

> *He thrusts his briefcase into her hand, and goes into the bedroom, tearing off his clothes.* FLICK *starts to pack the files.*

How was the interview?

FLICK: Interview? It felt more like an inquisition.

TOM: [*off*] When are they showing it?

FLICK: Friday night.

TOM: [*off*] I'll have to miss it.

FLICK: So will I. Can you believe it, she asked me if I'd been unfaithful? Well, near enough.

*She listens for a response from the bedroom.*

Tom? She asked me—

TOM *re-enters, half-dressed.*

TOM: Have you seen my reading glasses?

FLICK: About fidelity.

TOM: What about fidelity?

FLICK: That's what she said. What kind of question is that?

TOM: Par for the course. Australian journos are only interested in dirt. If you brought them Simpson and his donkey, they'd be checking them for steroids. Have you seen them?

FLICK: What?

TOM: My reading glasses.

FLICK: By the bed.

*He goes back into the bedroom. She goes on packing.*

She was out for blood, I think. And she got it. She said the damned word, and I blushed. Would that show up on television? That will look great, won't it? What do you think about fidelity, Felicity? And… whoosh. Sunset over Pittwater.

TOM: [*off*] What did she ask about Jason?

FLICK: Do you remember when I used to blush all the time?

TOM: [*off*] What?

*He reappears with a suitcase which he dumps in the middle of the floor.*

What did you say?

FLICK: I said I used to blush, remember, at the drop of a—

TOM: About Jason.

FLICK: What?

TOM: She must have asked.

FLICK: Well, she didn't, Tom. There are other topics in the world.

*The telephone rings.* TOM *answers.*

TOM: Hi, Jason. Hang on. [*To* FLICK] Could you pack my razor?

   *She goes.*

Yes, I did... Yes, I did... Yes, I will... I said I will, Jase. I've cancelled that... because I don't want you talking to anyone without me there, Jason.

   FLICK *returns with the razor.*

And my swimmers?

   *She goes.*

Because we both know what happens... Yes, we do... Then cast your mind back to Monte Carlo...

   FLICK *returns with the swimmers.*

Monte Carlo airport, and a large glass of pomegranate juice... All right, guava juice... You didn't spill it, you threw it over them... Well, it's not the usual way to end a press conference... Jason, you... [*To* FLICK] Toilet-bag.

   *She goes into the bedroom.*

No, not you, Jason, I'm talking to Flix. Jason, you don't seem to... I'm not arguing the point, mate... No, and that's an order... Beverly Hills Hotel...Yes, I will. I've got a plane to catch, Jason. See you in a week.

   *He hangs up as* FLICK *returns with the toilet-bag.*

FLICK: He's not going with you?
TOM: No.
FLICK: Why not?
TOM: Promise not to laugh?
FLICK: Promise.
TOM: His clairvoyant advised him not to fly this week.

   FLICK *starts to giggle.* TOM *laughs with her for a moment.*

Who'd have kids? Okay, let's go. Diary.
FLICK: His clairvoyant. In the briefcase.
TOM: A toilet-bag.
FLICK: In the suitcase.
TOM: What would I do without you?

FLICK: You'd buy another toilet-bag in L.A. There are six in the bathroom cupboard. I like the cunning little fake-fur number. Or is it a sporran?

*The phone rings.*

TOM: If that's him again—

FLICK: You're not here. [*Answering*] Hello? Jean-Luc, hi. He has? Oh, poor old Doog… oh, Christ. So I have…Yes, I will…I will. Bye.

*She hangs up.*

Tom, I'm sorry. Disaster. I've given Sharon the evening off, and now Doog's come down with a migraine. I'm going to have to go down to the restaurant and cook.

TOM: Oh, shit, Flix.

FLICK: You'll make it, don't worry.

TOM: I wanted you to drive me.

FLICK: You can call a cab, can't you?

TOM: I thought we'd have some time to talk.

FLICK: About what?

TOM: Just talk. You've been so busy—

FLICK: I've been so busy?

TOM: Yes. I've hardly seen you.

FLICK: Give me a break!

TOM: All right. I'll do just that.

FLICK: What?

TOM: You want a break? Come with me.

FLICK: What?

TOM: Come to L.A.

FLICK: To L.A. for a break? You must be mad!

TOM: Maybe so. But it'll give us some time together.

FLICK: You really think so?

TOM: Go on, pack a bag.

FLICK: I can't, Tom.

TOM: It's not what you would have said a couple of years ago.

FLICK: A couple of years ago I hadn't seen you in action.

TOM: Come on, you deserve a break.

FLICK: And so do you, but can you take one?

TOM: Sure. A couple of days for business, then—

FLICK: We tried this already, remember?

TOM: Did we? When?

FLICK: Several times.

TOM: Name one.

FLICK: Mexico City. Two days for business, then the wonders of Popocatapetl and Ixtywhatsis. Fat chance. Five days of the wonders of Casa del Hilton. I don't want to sit in a hotel room and watch you on the telephone. I can get all that at home.

TOM: Don't lay that on me. I've been home for a whole, week.

FLICK: A whole week!

TOM: No, longer. Nine days since Monte Carlo, and—

FLICK: Nine days. A second honeymoon. We even finished a tube of toothpaste together. That's what I call stability.

TOM: Okay, the days have been busy, but every night—

FLICK: Every night, you're conked out asleep in front of the television—

TOM: Waiting for you to knock out two thousand words on extra-virgin olive oil and Baltic vinegar.

FLICK: Balsamic. And let me remind you about last Wednesday night, Tom. You were cooking dinner, remember? I was going to come home and there'd be something smoking away in the Weber, and something cooling the ice, and we'd sit out there and watch the sun set over the water.

TOM: And you didn't get home till after dark.

FLICK: Granted, but by the time I was out of the shower, you were on the phone to Tokyo.

TOM: It was a crisis.

FLICK: It was one hour and ten minutes by the clock, followed by another hour with that old hippy in the mountains.

TOM: That old hippy knows more about deep tissue therapy than anyone in the country.

FLICK: Gosh.

TOM: He gave some very helpful advice.

FLICK: While our dinner dried out—

TOM: Which has worked wonders for Jason.

FLICK: Then it wasn't a wasted evening.

TOM: If the call hadn't been important—

FLICK: It's always important, and it always comes—

*The telephone rings. He answers.*

In the middle of something unimportant.

TOM: Hello?

FLICK: Like our lives.

TOM: It's for you. Dougal.

FLICK: Oh.

*She takes the phone.*

Doog… How are you feeling, baby? Jean-Luc called me… No, don't, sweetheart. We'll manage. Just stay lying down… Don't worry…Yes, I will… Love you. Bye.

*She hangs up.*

TOM: You sure he's not trying one on?

FLICK: Doog? Never. He was worried that I couldn't handle Saturday on my own. He's forgotten what I used to handle…

TOM: I haven't. You were a whizz.

FLICK: Was I?

*They glance at one another. Pause.*

You'd better call that cab. I'll pick you up, promise. Leave your flight number on the phone pad.

*She kisses him.*

TOM: I'll take the car.

FLICK: Suit yourself. See you for dinner on Saturday.

TOM: Sunday.

FLICK: Sunday? You said a week.

TOM: And one day.

FLICK: Cut the day. Come back Saturday.

TOM: Can't do it, Flix.

FLICK: Course you can.

TOM: Big dinner, Friday night, L.A. time.

FLICK: Skip it.

TOM: I wish I could. But it's the house rules in California. First the sushi, then the contract.

FLICK: You can't change it?

TOM: They're flying in from everywhere. It's quite a big deal, this one.

FLICK: A big deal. Well, so is—
TOM: [*over her*] Jason's going to be a very rich...
     [*registering*] What? So's what?
FLICK: Never mind. Sunday week.

> *She waves and heads out the door.*

TOM: Sunday week. Hang on. Reading-glasses...
FICK: By the bed.

> TOM *runs into the bedroom. She goes out, closing the door as* TOM *re-enters. He picks up his bags, and is hurrying out the door, when there is a ring from within the briefcase. He opens it, and answers a mobile phone inside it.*

TOM: Yes? Jason... because I'm not in the car, I'm still trying to get out the door. No, I won't, Jason... no, I won't... because I'm not into all that...I don't care if I she's got a swimming-pool... She's not my speed, Jason... No, Jason... Jason... All right... I will... I'll call her... I said I'll call her... No, I don't, but I can look it up... All right, give it to me...

> *Balancing the mobile phone, he extracts a small diary and pen, takes out his reading glasses, and jots down a number.*

Yes, I will, I'll call her... but Jason, not a word about this to anyone, all right?

> *He hangs up, puts his glasses away and picks up his keys. He picks up his bags and goes out the front door.*


## SCENE TWO

*A week later.* FLICK *sings cheerfully in the kitchen.*

FLICK: [*singing off*]
> Shall we gather at the river
> The beautiful, the beautiful, the river...

> *She enters, in an apron, and puts down a vase of Australian native flowers.*

> Shall we gather at the river...

*She glances out at the view.*

Yes, we shall.

*She goes on half-singing, half-humming quietly as she lays the table.*

> Yes, we will gather at the river,
> The beautiful, the beautiful, the river,
> Yes we will gather at the river,
> That flows by the throne of—

*The doorbell rings.*

Oh, God!

*She takes off the apron, and hurries to the front door, opening it to see* BUNTY *in a tennis dress.*

Oh, Bunty.

BUNTY: Darling. I was worried.

FLICK: Worried?

BUNTY: Are you all right, Felicity?

FLICK: I'm fine.

BUNTY: Truly? I dropped into the restaurant and spoke to Jean-Luc… oh, those eyelashes.

FLICK: Yes, they do more work than he does.

BUNTY: And he said you'd taken the night off, and naturally I feared the worst…

FLICK: What worst?

*The phone rings. She answers.*

Hello? Dougal? I said no calls, Doog… Lobster… just grilled with…

BUNTY *murmurs approval.*

Oh, Doog, what's wrong? … Oh, he wouldn't… He wouldn't leave you, he cares too much about…Oh, he did… He said that? Well, I'm sure you can work it out. Jean-Luc is young, Doog, and… Oh, yes, he's lovely—

BUNTY: Gorgeous.

FLICK: Gorgeous, my mother says gorgeous. Bye. [*She hangs up.*] Jean-Luc is a shameless little trollop.

BUNTY: Darling, boys can't be trollops.

FLICK: Yes they can, specially with eyes that blue. Mother, I'm a bit pressed at the moment.

BUNTY: You don't mean depressed?

FLICK: No, I mean busy.

BUNTY: You looked thoroughly miserable last night.

FLICK: Last night? Oh. Last night.

BUNTY: And then that awful review in the *Herald* this morning. I knew you'd be upset. We certainly were.

FLICK: We?

BUNTY: The girls at tennis. They felt so sorry for you.

FLICK: Mother, it was a television interview, not a firing squad.

BUNTY: Don't snap, Felicity, I came to cheer you up.

FLICK: I don't need cheering up!

BUNTY: [*seeing the table set*] Well, at least Tom's back tonight.

FLICK: No, tomorrow.

BUNTY: But darling! Isn't it your anniversary?

FLICK: You remembered?

BUNTY: And Tom didn't? Oh, men never do. You should remind him.

FLICK: He still couldn't have been here. Jason-talk in L.A.

BUNTY: Oh! What a pity. There's something so romantic about this last twilight before the clocks go back. Look at that sunset. It's telling you something, darling.

FLICK: It's telling me it's time to start dinner.

BUNTY: It's time to start your family.

FLICK: Take it up with Tom, mother. Now—

BUNTY: It takes a little effort on both sides.

FUCK: These days it takes a little effort to get in a handshake, let alone anything that might lead to conception.

*The telephone rings.*

Damn! [*She answers brusquely.*] Hello? Oh, Josh! You're lost? Where are you?… You're doing fine. No, stay on Barrenjoey… Yes, on the left, then the little park, the boat-ramp, then next street to the right…You got it. Get a move on. I want you here before the light goes… I mean before sunset… you'll see why. Bye.

*She hangs up and goes into the kitchen.* BUNTY *starts to polish the wine-glasses.*

BUNTY: Unusual name these days.

FLICK: [*off*] I suppose it is.

BUNTY: Joss, as in Jocelyn?

FLICK: [*off*] What?

BUNTY: I said Joss, as in Jocelyn?

> FLICK *enters carrying finger-bowls and a small American flag which she plants as a centre-piece.*

FLICK: What?

BUNTY: Is her name Jocelyn?

FLICK: Who?

BUNTY: The girl who's coming—

> *She sees the flag.*

Oh, she's American?

FLICK: American, yes, but—

BUNTY: Someone from your exchange year!

FLICK: That's right.

BUNTY: How lovely. You didn't tell me.

FLICK: I didn't know. I got a call at the restaurant at lunchtime.

BUNTY: You're sure she likes lobster? Some don't. What's her other name, by the way?

FLICK: What makes you think it's a her?

BUNTY: I don't think there are too many boys called Jocelyn.

FLICK: I suppose not.

BUNTY: Jocelyn what?

FLICK: Makepeace.

BUNTY: Makepeace? You're making that up.

FLICK: I'm not.

BUNTY: Jocelyn Makepeace, what an unusual name. Perhaps I'll stay and say hello.

FLICK: No, Bunty.

BUNTY: Oh, darling, hands across the water. They had you for a whole year.

FLICK: No, Bunty.

BUNTY: You're not ashamed of me, Felicity? I'm not your average North Shore widow, you know. I'm still active.

FLICK: I know.

BUNTY: And I have published.

FLICK: Bunty, you're a wonder. Now off you go.

BUNTY: I'd hate to think the *Herald* was right about you this morning. Spiky, they called you, darling.

FLICK: I read it.

BUNTY: Spiky and tense and surprisingly unsettled. They're nicer than that about Mr Keating. But you did come across like that. And the tone of some of those questions! That nun they had on last week, the entomologist, lovely serene face. They didn't ask her about fidelity.

FLICK: They asked me.

BUNTY: And now they all know, the girls at tennis and everyone.

FLICK: That I've been faithful to my husband?

BUNTY: That you haven't.

FLICK: But I have. You heard me.

BUNTY: Felicity, you blushed deep scarlet when the word was mentioned.

FLICK: That wasn't a blush.

BUNTY: The reception in Pymble is perfect.

FLICK: I mean, not that sort of blush, it was… look, Bunty, I've got to open some oysters.

> FLICK *goes into the kitchen.*

BUNTY: Is she one of those gorgeous blonde California girls? Felicity? Was she?

> FLICK *returns with oysters, a knife and a platter.*

With pom-poms?

FLICK: What?

BUNTY: Those girls at the football matches, jumping up and down…

FLICK: Cheerleaders.

BUNTY: Yes, was she a cheerleader? Big and blonde, I can just see her. Big in the bust—

FLICK: Mother—

BUNTY: All that work with the pom-poms. And perfect teeth.

FLICK: [*steering* BUNTY *to the door*] Perfect.

BUNTY: Fluoride, of course, they were onto it years before us. The Americans have led the world in oral hygiene. She sounds like a delight. I'm sorry I won't be meeting her.

FLICK: [*opening the door*] Well, I'm planning a quiet reunion.

BUNTY: Good. I'm having a quiet night with Bill Collins. It's his sincerity I love. I always feel he's there in the room with me, watching and enjoying.

> *She waves and goes, closing the door.* FLICK *takes a tape from the top of the VCR, inserts it and starts it. She opens the oysters as she watches.*

INTERVIEWER: Yes, I am surprised. To hear you talk about being lonely. I mean, your husband—

FLICK: [*on TV*] We agreed we aren't going to discuss him.

INTERVIEWER: Right. But he's in a high-pressure career—

FLICK: [*on TV*] Which we're also not going to discuss.

INTERVIEWER: Right. But your careers give each of you a certain public profile. I thought being alone might be a sort of asylum.

FLICK: Oh, please!

FLICK: [*on TV*] Oh, please! I thought I only thought that.

INTERVIEWER: Okay. Your husband's away a lot. Do you have any special understanding about that?

FLICK: [*on TV*] Yes, we've agreed to remember each other's first names.

INTERVIEWER: What about fidelity?

FLICK: No blush. There's no blush.

FLICK: [*on TV*] About the concept?

INTERVIEWER: Yes. Do you believe in it?

FLICK: There's a flush.

FLICK: [*on TV*] Yes, I do.

INTERVIEWER: But are there circumstances in which you would allow yourselves to be—

FLICK: [*on TV*] I can only answer for myself!

FLICK: And there's a blush. Sunset over Pittwater.

> *The doorbell rings.* FLICK *switches off the VCR, and goes to answer it. She stops, smelling her hands.*

Just a minute!

> *She runs into the kitchen, then returns to open the door.* JOSH *stands there with wine and flowers. They look at each other in silence for a moment.*

JOSH: Shall we gather at the river?

> *They embrace.*

Well we done it. We done gathered at the river.

FLICK: It's called Pittwater. Not quite a river.

JOSH: [*indicating the deck*] But quite a view. And so is this. God damn. You look—

FLICK: Thirty-seven.

> *He presents the flowers and wine.*

Thank you.

> *She looks at the label.*

You certainly splashed out.

JOSH: Well, it's a step up from cherry Cokes.

> *She gives* JOSH *the bottle and opener and goes into the kitchen, returning with a vase, as* JOSH *opens the wine.*

And I made it before sunset.

FLICK: Wasn't it worth it? It ends tonight. I mean… summer time. Even in Queensland. Though they don't like daylight saving up there. It puts the cattle off their feed. I can't believe this… we haven't seen one another in twenty years, and I'm telling you about the Queensland dairy industry. Anyway, it's my favourite night of the year.

JOSH: Then I'm glad to be sharing it. [*He hands her a glass of wine.*] Cheers.

FLICK: Cheers. But Josh, how on earth did you find me?

JOSH: You found me. I was in a bar last night. There was a TV set—

FLICK: Oh, no!

JOSH: Somebody asked the barman to put on the tennis. He pressed a button, and, pfft, there you were. I heard you say restaurant, and, pfft, Becker and Lendl.

FLICK: And you persuaded them to turn back to me?

JOSH: No, I watched Becker and Lendl. But after the game, I called up some fancy restaurant. I figured if you were talking on TV you weren't slinging hash in some diner. I said, how do I find Felicity Hayes? They said call the Whale Beach Cafe. You look good on TV.

FLICK: I felt like a fool.

JOSH: Kind of a heavy interview, huh?

FLICK: I thought you only heard me say restaurant?

JOSH: No, I did bear them asking you about being lonely. They went in close on your face, and—

FLICK: Pfft, Boris and Ivan.

JOSH: Battling out the tie-breaker. So how did you answer?

FLICK: Wait till it's out on video. You're a tennis fan these days?

JOSH: I'm crazy for it.

FLICK: You hated all that stuff back then.

JOSH: Back then we hated lots of things. L.B.J.—

FLICK: The military-industrial complex—

JOSH: The John Birchers, the D.A.R.—

FLICK: Saluting the flag—

JOSH: Oh, no! The flag we loved. One flag, anyway.

*He sees the little flag on the table-centre.*

Hey! There it is.

*He holds it up. She is puzzled.*

You mean you don't remember?

*She shakes her head.*

Ours was bigger than this. Big enough for two.

FLICK: Oh! Oh, yes! Yes! It was as itchy as hell, and I got the imprint of a couple of stripes on my bum.

JOSH: What, no stars?

FLICK: Just the stripes.

JOSH: Maybe you saw the stars.

FLICK: I saw the ceiling of your parents' cabana. What a low act, taking my virginity on top of Old Glory.

JOSH: Well, you took mine.

FLICK: What! You told me—

JOSH: I was lying. I was the last virgin in the senior class. That rubber in my wallet was so old I practically had to iron it.

FLICK: But you were so patronising. You told me the political gesture was more important than the act itself.

JOSH: The act itself was more fun.

FLICK: Maybe for you.

JOSH: Hey!

FLICK: It's all right, Josh. The second time was terrific. And it got better. And better. Well, we've certainly moved on from the Queensland dairy industry. See, the light's nearly gone.

*There is a rumble on the roof.*

Possum time.

JOSH: Possums in the suburbs?

FLICK: Not the suburbs, the Peninsula. They live in these trees, and every night they like to run across the roof. It's the only drawback to living up here. Everything else is pretty perfect.

JOSH: Perfect? Wow. Hey, is that a gym in your basement?

FLICK: Well, it's a work-out room.

JOSH: So now you're a fitness freak? We used to laugh at all those jocks at high school.

FLICK: Brad… Biff…

JOSH: Blair… Buck…

FLICK: Butch. And the girls! Those cheerleaders, with their perfect teeth and their pom-poms… two bits, four bits, six bits, a dollar, all for Corona, stand up and holler! Coro-na! All of them smiling up at the bleachers like a showroom full of Cadillacs. Let me get the line-up. Don't help me… Cindy… Mary-Jo… Donna Sue…And, oh, the pick of the bunch, what was her name? The best teeth, the best figure, every jock's dream of bliss. You remember.

JOSH: It was twenty years ago!

FLICK: You must remember. Homecoming queen. Baton twirler. Christmas.

JOSH: Christmas?

FLICK: Something like. Carol? Noelle? Holly! That's it, Holly. Holly Magnuson. You remember Holly.

JOSH: Holly. Oh, sure.

FLICK: They were all hanging out for Holly. And which one of them did she marry? Brad? Biff? Buck?

JOSH: None of them. She married me.

FLICK: Oh. Well, she was a very remarkable girl. I used to stand next to her in choir. It was a big voice, very big. Chest resonance, I suppose. And she can't have thought too much of Brad and Biff and Buck if she went and married a man called Joshua Makepeace.

JOSH: Yeah.

FLICK: Josh, I'm drowning. Eat an oyster and save me.

*She offers the platter. He takes an oyster and eats it.*

JOSH: Mm. Great. Very good. What did you do to these?

FLICK: I opened them. It makes eating easier.

JOSH: So, you're a famous cook.

FLICK: I wouldn't say famous.

JOSH: You were on TV.

FLICK: For the first and last time. A series on six women of achievement, quote unquote, called *Tough At The Top*. Tough is right. All I got from it was a tension headache and a roasting in this morning's paper. Now you. The whole story, please.

JOSH: Well, no surprises. I'm teaching history.

FLICK: High school?

JOSH: Stanford.

FLICK: I beg your pardon. A university lecturer.

JOSH: Professor.

FLICK: Professor Makepeace. What's your field?

JOSH: People who screwed on the American flag.

FLICK: You never told me we were part of a tradition.

JOSH: *Radical Theories and Movements, Twentieth Century, U.S.*

FLICK: I thought this generation didn't need all that.

JOSH: They need entertaining. And I'm entertaining. *Sacco and Vanzetti*, the mini-series.

FLICK: And what brings you to Sydney, Professor?

JOSH: Somebody liked my Roosevelt book and asked me to come give a paper on the New Deal. I gave it, they loved it. And a barman turned on Becker and Lendl and, pfft—

FLICK: Here you are.

JOSH: Nice timing, too. I fly out tomorrow night.

FLICK: You have to?

JOSH: I teach a class Monday. *Sacco and Vanzetti* live.

FLICK: I'm sorry. I'd like you to have met Tom.

JOSH: Tom?

FLICK: My husband. He's back from L.A. tomorrow night.

JOSH: Your husband.

FLICK: Yes.

JOSH: You're married.

FLICK: Well, yes. You're surprised.

JOSH: No, it's just… well, on TV, you seemed sort of lonely, and, I don't know, sad.

FLICK: Married people don't ever get sort of lonely and I don't know, sad? Are things that good with Holly?

JOSH: Hey! You still use your own name, okay? And anyway, you didn't tell me.

FLICK: You didn't ask me.

JOSH: How long?

FLICK: Seven years. Seven years exactly.

JOSH: Exactly?

FLICK: It's our anniversary today.

JOSH: [*whistling*] And he's in L.A.? Some anniversary.

FLICK: He's a very busy man.

> *The phone rings.* FLICK *answers it.*

Dougal. No, I wouldn't want you to do that… Well, because we'd miss you… Anyway, I believe it takes forever, and your whole life flashes before your… Stay with us, and work through it… Yes, you can, Doog. You can. Now dry those tears, and back to work. Bye.

> *She hangs up.*

JOSH: Who was that!

FLICK: Just my chef about to throw himself off the jetty. I've taken my last phone call. Tell me about Holly.

JOSH: You know about Holly.

FLICK: I remember her, but I guess twenty years have seen some changes. She's not still a cheerleader. Is she?

JOSH: She teaches aerobics.

FLICK: I can see that. Kids?

JOSH: One. Kelly. She's ten. And you?

FLICK: No. Not yet. I'd like one. We tried, once. And then… well, things got hectic. You live on campus?

JOSH: No, in the city, in San Francisco.

FLICK: Holly works downtown?

JOSH: She… no, she works out of town.

FLICK: Oh. Where?
JOSH: Uh… Boston.
FLICK: Boston. That's… that's out of town all right.
JOSH: We're divorced.
FLICK: Oh. You didn't tell me.
JOSH: You didn't ask me.
FLICK: Well, I wouldn't, would I?

> *The phone rings.*

Damn!

> JOSH *answers for her.*

JOSH: Good evening. You are now entering the *Twilight Zone.*

> *He hums the theme, and hangs up.*

'Ah want to spick to Felice.'
FLICK: Jean-Luc. My head waiter. Dougal's other half. Thank you. So, it didn't work out with Holly?
JOSH: We had a good couple of years… well, a good couple of months… well, the honeymoon was great. Hey, Flicka, can we start over?
FLICK: Flicka. Nobody's called me that since you.
JOSH: They don't call you Felicity!
FLICK: Only my mother. There's something about my name that makes everyone else dangerously creative. Flip, Flick, Lizard, Blister. I answer to anything. How do you mean, start over?
JOSH: I mean, junk the past, just for now.
FLICK: It's hard, Josh. You're it. You're that year, the year that turned my head around. From Presbyterian Ladies' College to Beach Blanket High School. From Ancient Airs and Dances with the recorder group to Led Zeppelin with you.
JOSH: At least we can call time out.

> *The possums run on the roof. He looks up.*

Cool it, fellas. How are things here and now?
FLICK: For me? Busy. Okay.
JOSH: [*refilling their glasses*] That good? So tell me.
FLICK: I have a restaurant. It's over the hill. I mean literally. That way. In an old cottage on Whale Beach. I cleaned down the walls, and planted a garden, and turned it into a place I might like to sit in, and

cooked the food I might like to eat. I found Dougal, we found a way of making it work, and...

JOSH: People came.

FLICK: People come. It's nice. It's where I met Tom. He was a regular.

JOSH: Was?

FLICK: Well, now, he travels a lot... he doesn't have the time.

JOSH: What takes him away so much?

FLICK: Business.

JOSH: What, he's in exports?

FLICK: Yes. Exports.

JOSH: You're lying, Flicka, I remember that look. Oh, God, I'm sorry, it isn't... organised crime?

FLICK: I wouldn't call it organised. He is in exports. Sports exports.

JOSH: As in hockey pucks? Tennis balls?

FLICK: As in tennis players.

JOSH: He manages tennis players.

FLICK: One. One player.

JOSH: Who!

FLICK *silently lifts up the glossy cover of a magazine, to reveal a photo of* JASON *in motion.*

You're putting me on.

FLICK *shakes her head.*

Holy shit. Jason Strutt. He manages Jason Strutt. He coaches Jason Strutt. This is incredible. You made him sound like a drug-runner, and he manages Jason Strutt. He's Tom Finn!

FLICK *nods.*

Jason Strutt. Holy shit. I mean, Wimbledon, that was poetry, there hasn't been a final like that since... Hoad, Gonzales, Borg, you name it. I saw him at Flushing Meadow, paid nearly the whole damn advance on the Roosevelt book for two seats centre court, and... well, forget Roosevelt, forget the New Deal, that was history! Jason Strutt. And you didn't want to tell me. Why?

FLICK: I thought you might do what you've just done.

JOSH: What?

FLICK: Have an orgasm on my floor.

JOSH: Flicka, I'm impressed. The guy is living history.

FLICK: Then help yourself. We have all his games on video.

JOSH: I have all his games on video.

FLICK: No you don't. We go back to fourteen. A high school tournament in Wollongong. Tom discovered him. On our honeymoon. Seven years ago tomorrow. We were driving south to Bermagui, but Tom got a hot tip, and suddenly we didn't need a honeymoon. We had a kid ready-made, wrapped in sweatbands, bouncing three feet behind the baseline.

JOSH: Jason plays the net.

FLICK: Now he does, after seven years of blood, sweat and Staminade.

JOSH: Something tells me you don't like him.

FLICK: I don't like people's eyes glazing over when they find out I was wet-nurse to a living legend. And I don't like what it's done to my life.

JOSH: You have your restaurant. You have Dougal.

FLICK: Yes, I have Dougal, if he hasn't drowned himself.

*The phone rings. She starts.*

He's drowned himself.

JOSH: Let it ring, Flicka.

FLICK: What if he has drowned himself?

JOSH: Then he won't be calling.

FLICK: What if he's drowned Jean-Luc? No, that would be too much to hope for. I'm not going down there, boys. Sort it out yourselves.

*The phone stops.*

Well!

JOSH: Attagirl. Have another drink.

*The phone rings again.*

FLICK: It could be mayhem down there.

JOSH: Flicka! Is this our night, or is it?

FLICK: Well, yes, it's our night.

JOSH: Then no more Dougal and Jean-Luc?

FLICK: No more Jason Strutt?

*JOSH nods. The phone stops. Pause. Possums can be heard on the roof.*

JOSH: And no more possums!

> *Sudden silence.* FLICK *is impressed.*

It's a beautiful evening.

FLICK: Now, that lobster.

> *She goes towards the kitchen.*

JOSH: And the whole town is quiet.

FLICK: For the moment, at least.

JOSH: Can you hear it?

FLICK: Hear what?

JOSH: Hear the hush. Can you hear it, Lily?

> *Silence.*

FLICK: [*assuming American accent*] Yes, I can.

JOSH: Do you think… do you think we can be this happy always, Lily?

> FLICK *looks uncertain.* JOSH *prompts.*

Mama says…

FLICK: Thank you. Mama says it never lasts.

JOSH: What if it's for us that the whole town is quiet, Lily?

FLICK: It's quiet… um…

> *She drops the accent.*

What was his name?

JOSH: Amos.

FLICK: It's quiet because it's sleeping, Amos.

JOSH: No, it's quiet for us, Lily. I know that.

FLICK: How do you remember?

JOSH: No! Go on, please. Crocus.

FLICK: Oh. I saw a crocus today.

JOSH: It's the first night of spring, Lily. Let's stay out here alone, and see if it is for us… this hush, this scent on the breeze, this moon.

> *He goes to kiss her. She avoids it. It is not clear whether this moment is in the remembered play.*

FLICK: There's no moon, Amos.

JOSH: There will be. Grandpa says it's in the almanac.

> *He kisses her.*

FLICK: I was never out this late before. And yet—

*She signals for help.*

JOSH: Churchyard. Dreams.

FLICK: And yet I been here before, in this churchyard. Waiting for the moon to rise. I been here, in my dreams.

*He is close to her. She breaks away.*

JOSH: You stopped.

FLICK: That's where the preacher's wife came on. My one and only appearance on a public stage.

JOSH: You loved it.

FLICK: I loved kissing you in front of the whole school, I didn't love acting. You were the one that loved it. All that talk about Ho Chi Minh and the Chicago Seven, but Josh Makepeace was a romantic at heart.

JOSH: Bullshit!

FLICK: You remember every word of that play!

JOSH: It's a great anti-war statement. A national classic. You cut my big speech.

FLICK: No, the preacher's wife brings on the basket and talks about her dead child.

JOSH: No, first the moon comes up, and I kiss you again.

*He kisses her on the cheek.*

Lily. I'm eighteen come April, and when that day comes I'll walk down that road, and I'll cross the bridge and sign my name, and they'll send me off some place far away. But I ain't going alone. You're going with me, Lily.

FLICK: No, Andy.

JOSH: Amos.

FLICK: Amos.

JOSH: The crocuses will bloom, and soon will come the harvest, and then the time for storing and setting indoors. But you'll go through all that time like a sleep-walker. For you'll be with me, wherever. You and this night, and this hush, and this moon.

FLICK: This is a national classic now, is it?

JOSH: It was then.

FLICK: Well, you were very good. Wonderful, in fact.

JOSH: On the stage?

FLICK: On the stage. And off it.

*Pause.*

JOSH: Summer time ends tonight, huh? And the clocks go back.

*She nods.*

We have an extra hour. Between tonight and tomorrow. When does your husband fly in?

FLICK: Josh…

JOSH: When?

FLICK: I told you, tomorrow night. Round seven-thirty.

JOSH: I fly out at six-thirty.

FLICK: What are you saying, Josh?

JOSH: Look, I saw you on TV—

FLICK: Oh, why did I do it!

JOSH: And you looked very lonely.

FLICK: For a moment, yes. Then pfft, Becker and Lendl.

JOSH: Your face showed me something, even then. Even now.

FLICK: Like what?

JOSH: Like a kind of void in your life.

FLICK: Thank you. And you came up here to fill it?

JOSH: Heavy!

FLICK: Hea-vy! Wow, put on Led Zeppelin, and pass me the weed.

JOSH: Actually, I did bring some with me…

FLICK: These days it gives me hiccoughs. Look, neither of us is seventeen.

JOSH: So?

FLICK: We haven't just seen *2001* stoned. This is not your parents' cabana.

JOSH: We do have an American flag.

FLICK: Oh, Josh! You were wonderful. But now… it's twenty years on, and another country altogether.

JOSH: I heard your voice on the phone. You were excited. You wanted me to come.

FLICK: Because you were here. You called, and…

JOSH: And you put the flag out.

FLICK: As a memento. Josh, I have a husband.

JOSH: Who's out of town for your anniversary. You are lonely, aren't you?

FLICK: Well… sometimes. But…

JOSH: But what?

FLICK: I'm okay. I'm prepared to wait—

JOSH: For what!

FLICK: For Tom to settle down. For Jason Strutt to be bought by Alan Bond. Or vice versa. For a life with somebody.

JOSH: A life with somebody?

FLICK: This is turning into tennis, Josh. Wham, whap, volley—

JOSH: Set point. I want to stay the night.

FLICK: I asked you for dinner.

JOSH: I'll make you breakfast.

FLICK: You're the only person I've ever met who cooks worse than my mother.

JOSH: I give good breakfast. Breakfast is the first thing you conquer after a divorce.

FLICK: Oh, God, Josh. I… I don't do this. Never. Not once in seven years.

JOSH: Lack of opportunity?

FLICK: No. I know a lot of men.

JOSH: Like Dougal and Jean-Luc?

FLICK: Straight men, too. Though I will admit, in this town, the straight single man is a rare and precious thing. We sometimes sacrifice them at dawn on North Head to make the crops fruitful.

JOSH: Promise me one thing?

FLICK: I hate people saying that. What?

JOSH: You'll stop making jokes to deflect anything serious?

FLICK: This isn't serious, Josh. You don't seriously want this, you want a night in 1969.

JOSH: And don't you?

*Silence. The phone rings. They stand in silence till it rings off.*

FLICK: Well, maybe one night.

*He moves towards her.*

No, I can't, Josh. It doesn't feel right.

JOSH: [*holding her*] Doesn't it?

FLICK: [*returning his embrace*] Oh, yes. Yes, it does.

JOSH: And when I called…?

FLICK: You're right. I was excited. And I think I did want this. I'm not even sure why.

JOSH: [*taking the phone off the hook*] Because you've been with me forever. You, and this night, and this hush…

STEPHANIE: [*off*] Fliss? Fliss?

> FLICK *and* JOSH *move apart as* STEPHANIE *enters at speed from one end of the deck.*

Fliss, thank Christ you're here.

> *She pours herself a glass of wine while talking, oblivious of* JOSH.

You know what that bastard has done to me now? Yes, I know. I know you said, 'Take it easy, Steph, go easy with this one.' But I thought, no, this is the one, Brendan's the one. I mean, Brendan, that should have been the giveaway, even if I'd missed the Miraculous Medal on the dashboard. But there he was, this vital, vibrant, caring man, who took three months to tell me his marriage was a sacrament, so even though he couldn't live without me, he couldn't live with me. Well, I could live with that, right? I could live with anything. Until tonight. I could live with the guilt, and the clock-watching, and the quick dash for the door to make it home before Bernadette gets back from her Ecumenical Tae Kwon Do group. I could live with being stood up for a Pentecostal Bushwalk. I can live with Brendan and Bernadette, I mean not live with Brendan because of Bernadette… well, because of Brendan, the gutless little Mick turd. I can live with anything but this. You know what he's done, Fliss? You know what Brendan has done? He has given me up for Lent.

FLICK: Steph, this is Josh.

STEPHANIE: Can you believe that? Given me up for Lent. Like I'm a box of chocolates.

FLICK: Josh, Stephanie.

STEPHANIE: That's it. A box of Darrell Lea chocolates, sitting on the shelf, not to be opened till Easter.

FLICK: Josh is a friend from California. Stephanie is my next-door neighbour.

STEPHANIE: I mean, not 'It's over, Steph', nothing that straight-forward. 'I've given you up for Lent, darling.'

*She eats an oyster.*

Fliss, what am I going to do?

FLICK: First you're going to say hello to my guest, then you're going to finish your drink and go. We're about to eat, Steph.

*She goes into the kitchen.* STEPHANIE *takes another oyster.*

JOSH: Hi.

STEPHANIE: You know, I did think Brendan was it. Intelligent, sensitive, no police record. And after all the ratbags that have come my way. I mean, Ken Willis. You knew Ken.

JOSH: No, I never did.

STEPHANIE: Well, you remember all that stuff in the papers. Did you know Frankie Snedden?

JOSH: Sorry.

STEPHANIE: Ex Manly CID. Took early retirement and went to work for Colonel Rabuka. And best of the lot, Sergei. Sergei Nicolayev, you knew him. Remember the beard and the fur coat?

JOSH: Afraid not.

STEPHANIE: You don't know anyone, do you?

*She takes another oyster.*

Sergei was the full Slav bit. Dirty collar, dirty fingernails, straight Stolichnaya for breakfast, the full bit. Black bread and long card games and lots of crying. I was in heaven. Then this old lady turns up looking for Sid. Sid Nicols. It's his Mum from Toukley. His Auntie Iris has died and left him a milk-bar at The Entrance. So he goes off to run the milk-bar at The Entrance. Das Vedanya, Sid. He was the first. But it's not as though I haven't learned. I've learned to look for integrity, sanity and balance. I haven't found them. I've found Ken Willis, the professional cheque-bouncer. Frank Snedden, who brought the poker-machine to Fiji. And now Brendan Kennelly, who has given me up for Lent.

*She drains her glass.*

This wine is piss. Of course, all white wine is piss at this hour of the evening.

FLICK *enters with two plates.*

FLICK: We are eating seafood, Steph.

STEPHANIE: I'm not eating fish during Lent. I'm not bowing to two thousand years of Mick superstition.

*She pours another glass of wine.*

What sort of seafood?

FLICK: Lobster. One lobster.

STEPHANIE: I'll stretch a point for lobster.

FLICK: No, Steph. You hold your ground.

*An oven bell rings in the kitchen.* FLICK *goes, signalling desperation to* JOSH. STEPHANIE *finishes the oysters.*

STEPHANIE: She's fantastic, isn't she? I would die without Fliss.

JOSH: Stephanie, I'm going to ask you a great favour.

STEPHANIE: Did you see her on TV? So brave. So straight. I only saw the first couple of minutes, actually. Brendan was over, and he had to watch Becker and Lendl before he gave me up for Lent. Are you married?

JOSH: Well, uh, no.

STEPHANIE: You're gay.

JOSH: Stephanie, I'm going to ask you to give us this evening on our own.

STEPHANIE: You're American.

JOSH: Yes, here on a very short visit, so—

STEPHANIE: Fliss didn't say. Mind you, she never says much. She's the most fantastic listener.

FLICK *comes in.*

FLICK: Finished your wine, Steph?

STEPHANIE: Yes, I'll go and get something drinkable.

FLICK & JOSH: [*together*] Stephanie—

STEPHANIE: No, it's no trouble. Geez, I'm glad you're home tonight. Hold the lobster, I'll be back in a flash.

*She goes out via the deck.*

FLICK: She will, too. Let's escape. We'll go down to the water for an hour.

JOSH: It's always water for you, isn't it? Kiss me.

FLICK: Let's get out of here first.

JOSH: Kiss me, please.

*There is a knock on the door.*

Back in a flash. She wasn't kidding.

FLICK: Wrong direction.

*She puts a finger to her lips.*

Shh! We'll get out this way.

JOSH: No, dammit, it's your house. Take the challenge!

*He calls out.*

Come in!

FLICK: What is this?

JOSH: America's contribution to history: gunboat diplomacy. Come in, whoever you are!

*He throws open the door.* BUNTY *stands there. She wears a smart dress and carries a canvas carry-bag.*

BUNTY: My goodness. That sounded exactly like Henry Fonda in *Young Mr Lincoln.*

FLICK: Mother, this is Joshua Makepeace.

BUNTY: Hello, Joshua. Jocelyn's husband?

FLICK: Yes.

JOSH: Yes.

BUNTY: Jocelyn and Joshua. That's lovely, but don't people get you confused?

JOSH: No, not since I took to wearing my hair this short.

*They laugh, a little too long.*

BUNTY: And where's Jocelyn?

FLICK: Taken ill.

BUNTY: But she rang—

FLICK: At the very last minute. Food poisoning.

BUNTY: Poor girl! I'm sorry to miss her. I brought her one of my stories.

*She produces gifts from her bag.*

And a tin of my special Walnut Surprise. But she won't be up to that, will she?

JOSH: I would say not.

BUNTY: She was a cheerleader, I believe.

JOSH: A cheerleader?

> *He glances at* FLICK, *who nods firmly at him.*

Yes, a cheerleader. Two bits, four bits, six bits, a dollar…'

BUNTY: Marvellous figure, I hear. Lovely teeth…

JOSH: Homecoming queen.

FLICK: Baton twirler.

JOSH: She was quite a gal, my wife, Jocelyn.

FLICK: I was just about to serve dinner, mother.

BUNTY: You were in Felicity's class too?

JOSH: Corona Beach High School Class of '69, Ma'am.

BUNTY: Bunty.

JOSH: Pardon me?

BUNTY: Bunty. Call me Bunty. So you were all friends?

FLICK: Inseparable.

BUNTY: You and Jocelyn and Joshua.

FLICK: [*fingers crossed*] Like that.

JOSH: [*fingers crossed*] Like that.

BUNTY: How lovely. All three of you?

BUNTY, FLICK & JOSH: [*together*] Like that.

> *They laugh, a little too long.*

BUNTY: It's very odd.

JOSH: Odd?

BUNTY: She isn't in the yearbook.

FLICK: The yearbook?

BUNTY: Your high school yearbook. I found it at home.

> *She produces a U.S. high school yearbook from the carry-bag.*

She was such a prominent sort of girl, but there's no mention of her.

JOSH: [*deftly taking the book*] Oh, but Bunky—

BUNTY: Bunty.

JOSH: Bunty. I guess you looked for Makepeace.

BUNTY: No, Joshua. I looked for Jocelyn, and there's no one of that name in your class. In the entire school. Could they have left her out?

FLICK: No! She changed her first name, too.

BUNTY: Oh! And what was it?

FLICK & JOSH: [*miraculously together*] Holly.

JOSH: Yes… Holly.

BUNTY: Holly. But that's such a pretty name, why would she change it?

JOSH: Look, here she is.

> *He shows* BUNTY *the book.*

Homecoming Queen Holly Magnuson with the Corona Beach Bulldogs.

FLICK: Brad. Biff. Bart. Blair. Buck.

BUNTY: You're making those up!

> *She looks.*

Oh, you're not. And here's Holly. What a gorgeous creature. That figure. Those teeth. And a natural blonde?

JOSH: Yes.

FLICK: [*simultaneously*] No.

BUNTY: Now, where are those pom-poms?

FLICK: Mother, I think Josh is getting hungry.

BUNTY: He can have a Walnut Surprise.

FLICK: No!

BUNTY: [*taking out the tin and opening it*] It won't spoil his dinner.

FLICK: I wouldn't bet on that.

BUNTY: You look like a big eater. Have one.

JOSH: Thank you.

> *He takes it. He turns a page of the yearbook, which* BUNTY *now holds.*

There she is again. Future Home-makers of America.

BUNTY: Oh, how lovely! And what a pretty apron.

> FLICK *disposes of the Walnut Surprise for* JOSH. BUNTY *looks up.*

You've finished that already?

JOSH: Delicious.

BUNTY: [*offering the tin*] Have another.

JOSH: Thank you.

> *He takes it, then turns another page, and points to a picture.*

And again. With the Marching Girls.

*He passes the Walnut Surprise again to* FLICK, *as* BUNTY *looks at the book.*

BUNTY: Oh, she was gorgeous.

JOSH: And still is.

*He signals to* FLICK *to go.*

BUNTY: You're a very lucky man, Joshua. I'd say she was fighting the boys off with a stick.

FLICK: I wouldn't.

JOSH *signals again.* FLICK *goes.*

JOSH: Bunty, I'm going to ask you a great favour.

BUNTY: Yes, you can have just one more.

*As* JOSH *opens his mouth to reply,* BUNTY *pops a Walnut Surprise into it.*

There. I'm so pleased they've hit the spot. Felicity and Tom will never touch them.

JOSH *struggles with the glutinous mass in his mouth.*

Do you have children, Joshua?

JOSH, *struggling, nods.*

How many?

*He holds up one finger.*

Just one. A little boy or a little girl?

JOSH: [*indistinctly*] Girl.

BUNTY: A little girl?

JOSH: [*free at last*] Yes. Kelly. She's ten. She… we left her back home.

BUNTY: Oh. And you're missing her tonight? You look quite tearful, Josh. And I'm not surprised. Holly back at the hotel with a wonky tummy, little Kelly back at home and only two of you to pick over old times. Never mind, we'll have a nice cheery night. I'd love to hear all the tales.

JOSH: Bunty. This favour—

BUNTY: [*putting the lid on the tin*] Josh, Felicity will never forgive me if I spoil your dinner.

*She replaces the receiver on the telephone.*

JOSH: I'm not here for dinner. I mean not just for dinner. I've come to… have a heart-to-heart.

BUNTY: With Felicity?

JOSH: With Felicity. Bunky… Bunty, Holly… I mean Jocelyn, and me… well, things have gone terribly wrong for us.

BUNTY: Well, yes, food poisoning for one.

JOSH: Worse. We've grown apart. It's like we're living on different sides of the continent. We haven't had breakfast together in years. There've been… I'm sorry, Bunty… other men.

BUNTY: Other men. My goodness, things have changed since 1969.

JOSH: And that's why I'm here. To reclaim the girl I loved in 1969.

BUNTY: Are you sure you've come to the right place?

JOSH: Oh, yes. She told you, we were—

BUNTY & JOSH: [*together, fingers crossed*] Like that.

BUNTY: Even so. Felicity's a splendid girl, but not one I'd turn to for marriage guidance. Last night on television was not a portrait of a happily married woman. Spiky, the *Herald* said. Spiky and tense and surprisingly unsettled.

JOSH: Unsettled. Right. Like me. She can empathise.

*He leads* BUNTY *towards the door.*

BUNTY: I do hope you can bring one another a little joy.

JOSH: I hope so too.

*He is manoeuvring* BUNTY *out the door when* STEPHANIE *enters from the deck with a bottle of red wine.*

STEPHANIE: Here's something with a bit more body than that piss you've been drinking.

BUNTY: Stephanie. Hello.

STEPHANIE: Hello, Mrs Hayes.

BUNTY: I've said you can call me Bunty, dear.

STEPHANIE: I couldn't call anyone Bunty.

*She starts to open the bottle.*

BUNTY: I'll leave the Walnut Surprise, Joshua. And the story for your little girl. We shouldn't be lingering, dear. They're about to have a good heart-to-heart.

STEPHANIE: They'd better not be, Fliss has asked me to dinner.

*She picks up* BUNTY*'s book.*

What's this?

BUNTY: One of my stories. I brought it for—

STEPHANIE: [*reading*] *Nyngan The Naughty Platypus...*

BUNTY: It's a good read for the adventurous ten-year-old.

STEPHANIE: Adventurous ten-year-olds don't read. They go down behind the bike-sheds with other adventurous ten-year-olds.

JOSH: [*offering the tin to* STEPHANIE] Have one, please.

STEPHANIE: [*taking one*] That's Brendan's problem. He never went down behind the bike-shed. A couple of sessions down there, and he could have shaken off all that Mick guilt about sex.

*She puts it in her mouth, then gags as she feels its effects.*

BUNTY: Sensitivity, Stephanie. We have an overseas visitor.

STEPHANIE *hurries off into the kitchen.*

She'll enjoy it, Joshua. It's an allegory. Nyngan doesn't want to share his creekbank. The review in the *North Shore Times* mentioned multiculturalism, which wasn't a conscious theme, but that's the power of literature.

JOSH: [*taking it*] It looks very nice.

BUNTY: I self-publish. *Mirramimma Press*, see? It's an Aboriginal word meaning wisdom from the treetops.

JOSH: Great. Now, Bunty—

STEPHANIE *comes out of the kitchen carrying another table-setting, which she lays.*

STEPHANIE: You know the only time we ever talk? On the phone, when he's at work. And when he's at work, I'm at work. It's my space, my time, but Brendan rings, and I have to drop everything and listen. Never mind the hour, never mind the client, never mind my career!

JOSH: What is your career, Stephanie?

STEPHANIE: I'm in stress management. I have a consultancy in Crows Nest, and a growing number of executive clients.

STEPHANIE *idly plays with the American flag, then she uproots it, leaving it on the table.*

But it won't go on growing if I have to leave a client in mid-stress every time Brendan phones to have his ego stroked by a woman he has just given up for Lent. Oh, men are such bastards!

BUNTY: Stephanie, our guest!

STEPHANIE: Oh, not him, he's gay.

BUNTY: Oh, Joshua. When you said other men, I didn't realise...

*The telephone rings.* JOSH *answers.*

JOSH: Hello.

FLICK *runs in from the kitchen.*

FLICK: That phone was off the hook!

JOSH: It's Dougal. He's resigning.

FLICK: At nine-thirty on a Saturday night?

*She grabs the phone.*

Doog, what's this? ... He didn't! ... You didn't! No, you're not resigning... just go outside and look at the moon on the water... Yes there is, a lovely full one... Some nice deep breaths, and put Jean-Luc on. [*To* BUNTY *and* STEPHANIE.] Look, the lobster will only run to two.

BUNTY: Oh, I'm not hungry.

STEPHANIE: I am. And I was asked to dinner.

FLICK: [*into phone*] Jean-Luc? You're fired... Yes, fired... Oh, I can. You'll soon find another line of work, with eyes that colour.

BUNTY: They are gorgeous. Deep blue. You should see them... well, perhaps you shouldn't, Joshua.

FLICK: I mean it. How's Doog? ... Still? Oh, God! Stop snivelling, Jean-Luc, and do something.

BUNTY: You mustn't scold him, darling, the poor boy's confused. Imagine crying in a second language.

*She takes the phone.*

Jean-Luc? Ici, c'est Bunty... Bunty, la mere de Felicity, oui. Oh, pauvre garcon. [*To* FLICK] See, darling, a little understanding works wonders.

FLICK: Bunty. Bunty, why don't you go down there!

*She and* JOSH *exchange glances.*

BUNTY: [*into telephone*] Un moment, Jean-Luc.

FLICK: Go down there, mother. They both need a little, understanding. Josh will see Stephanie home, and—

STEPHANIE: What about dinner!

FLICK: What about Brendan? When he calls you'll want to be by that phone.

STEPHANIE: When he calls? Easter's weeks away!

FLICK: But you're only a phone call away.

JOSH: He'll be feeling vulnerable by now. Give him the chance to show it.

BUNTY: [*into phone*] Jean-Luc, ne pleurez plus, cheri.

STEPHANIE: Yes, I will. One last chance.

> *She collects the red wine, and presses* FLICK*'s hand on her way past.*

Isn't it wonderful hearing a man use the word vulnerable? And wouldn't you know, he's gay?

> JOSH *leads her out.*

BUNTY: [*into phone*] Bunty viendra… yes, I'm coming down, Jean-Luc, like the Foreign Legion.

> *She hangs up.*

Oh, he laughed.

FLICK: Good for you, Bunty. You'll work wonders. Take the Walnut Surprise.

BUNTY: I couldn't darling. It was a gift.

FLICK: Their need is greater. And food is their field, after all.

BUNTY: I'll come back and report, shall I?

FLICK: Call me in the morning. I'm planning an early night.

BUNTY: I don't think so, darling. Joshua has some very big things to get off his chest.

> *She waves and goes out the front door.* FLICK *relaxes against it. She goes to the tape-deck and puts on something identifiably late sixties. She hums along as it starts to play. She fetches a bottle of white wine. She looks out along the deck, but sees no sign of* JOSH. *She adjusts the table setting, planting the flag again, smiling as she does so. There is a knock on the door. She opens it.* TOM *stands there, without luggage.*

TOM: Hi.

FLICK: Tom. This is Saturday. Isn't it?

TOM: I thought I'd come home early. Before the clocks go back.

FLICK: Oh. Where are your keys?

TOM: I think I left them in L.A. I've been calling all the way home but you've been engaged all night. You and I have some talking to do.

FLICK: Oh, do we? Yes, we do. [*With one eye on the deck*] Yes.

TOM: God, that song takes you back, doesn't it?

FLICK: Maybe a bit too far. Yes, a bit too far.

> *She switches it off.*

Tom—

TOM: You said we never talk, and you're right. I've done the deal. Jason is going to be a very rich boy.

FLICK: I didn't say we never talk about Jason.

TOM: This is not about Jason. I mean, the deal's in place, and that makes the rest of it simpler.

FLICK: The rest of it?

TOM: I met this… Oh, shit. You're not going to like this. You see, I met this woman in L.A.

FLICK: Oh?

TOM: Well, not met. I'd seen her before, with Jason. But he insisted that I get in touch with her again. I didn't really want to, but… I did. And we had this amazing rave—

FLICK: Tom, I'm not sure I can take this on board tonight.

TOM: Listen to me, please. She's made me come to terms with a lot of things about us.

FLICK: About us?

TOM: I mean… come to terms with me.

FLICK: What sort of terms?

TOM: Well, what I need out of life. But it's going to mean some big changes. I want…

FLICK: What? What!

TOM: I want to start my life again.

> JOSH *appears on the deck.*

JOSH: That's a woman who's not easy to get away from.

> *He sees* TOM.

TOM: What?

JOSH: Tom Finn.

TOM: Yes.

FLICK: And this is… I'm sorry, I've forgotten your name.

*They look at one another in confusion.*

END OF ACT ONE

# ACT TWO

*SCENE ONE*

TOM, FLICK *and* JOSH *are in the same positions, scarcely a moment later.*

JOSH: Josh. Josh Makepeace.

FLICK: I'm sorry. Very sorry.

JOSH: I'm a friend of Stephanie's.

FLICK: Yes, a friend of Stephanie's. I was just going to give them dinner. Is that right?

JOSH: Yes. Yes, that's right. We've been looking forward to it. I hear she's a great cook.

TOM: The best. You're from the States?

JOSH: Yes. Your wife raised the flag in my honour.

TOM: [*seeing it*] So she did.

FLICK: Tom's just in from the States himself, so you'll excuse him if he flakes.

TOM: I'm fine, Flix. I slept all the way on the plane. But I am ravenous.

FLICK: Oh. Good.

JOSH: Flix. That's an unusual name.

TOM: Short for Felicity. Why don't you go and hurry Steph along?

JOSH: Oh. Sure. If… uh… Felicity's ready.

FLICK: I think I'm just about ready for anything now.

JOSH: Boy, if I'd known I was going to get to meet Tom Finn…

*He goes out via the terrace.*

TOM: How did he know who I was?

FLICK: He's a tennis fan. I believe.

TOM: Shit. If there's one thing I don't want to talk about tonight it's tennis.

FLICK: You amaze me. Tom. This woman in Los Angeles—

TOM: Look, we'll feed those two quick-smart, and then we'll talk.

FLICK: I need to know now. Before they come back.

TOM: Flix, it's big stuff.

*There is a knock on the door.*

How many people are you expecting tonight?

*He opens the door.* JASON *stands there in expensive casual clothes, carrying a small bag.*

JASON: What's the story, Finno?

TOM: Jason.

JASON: You came back early.

FLICK: Hello, Jason.

JASON: Hello, Mrs Finn. [*To* TOM] What went wrong?

TOM: Nothing.

JASON: You shouldn't do this to me.

TOM: Do what?

JASON: Distort my rhythms like this. Today's been totally negative for me. I couldn't meditate, I couldn't go with the flow at physio—

TOM: Why, Jase?

JASON: I couldn't find you. I called the hotel, you'd checked out. I called Heidi—

TOM: Jason.

FLICK: Heidi?

JASON: And she said you'd come home. Oh, and you left your keys by the pool.

*His watch-alarm goes off.*

I have to eat.

FLICK: I only have one lobster!

JASON: I've brought my own food.

*He takes some small containers from his bag, and lays them on the table.*

FLICK: What's for dinner?

JASON: Azuki beans, shitaki, tofu, miso—

FLICK: That's not dinner, that's the cast of a Kung Fu movie.

JASON: [*settling to eat*] And what about the deal?

TOM: The deal's signed. Why are you here, Jason?

JASON: I suppose you've read the *Herald*, Mrs Finn?

FLICK: Today's? Yes, I have.

JASON: What do you think?

FLICK: Well, everyone's entitled to an opinion.

JASON: Even if it's totally negative? Did you show him?

FLICK: No, I didn't.

JASON: I've brought a copy.

*He brings one out of his bag.*

FLICK: Jason! Oh. The sport section.

JASON: Well, of course the sport section. Letters this big: 'Strutt's Comeuppance'.

TOM: [*grabbing it*] Let me see that!

*He looks in his pockets and briefcase.*

Oh, shit, my reading glasses. Don't tell me I left them…

FLICK: By Heidi's pool?

TOM: Could be. Read it for me, Flix.

FLICK: [*taking the paper from* TOM] 'Strutt's Comeuppance?' It does end with a question-mark. By Vin Barnett. 'Has Jason Strutt been on top of the heap too long for his own good? Wednesday's Tokyo tournament will be crucial for the Kiama Kid—

JASON: They've got to stop calling me that.

FLICK: 'Japanese prodigy Yoshi Yakimura is ranked only 23 in current seedings, but Nipponese training innovations have given him a style like something perfected by Nashua.'

TOM: Bullshit.

FLICK: 'Is Yoshi the one to beat Strutt? Last week's bad boy behaviour at Monte Carlo—

JASON: That was a bad line-call!

TOM: No, it wasn't.

JASON: Was. You got any yeast, Mrs Finn?

FLICK: Top shelf of the pantry cupboard.

> JASON *goes out crossly.*

Heard enough?

TOM: Yes, but go on.

FLICK: And the last thing you wanted to talk about tonight was tennis. Uh… 'Monte Carlo… the latest in a series of high-profile tantrums. Strutt holds his international ranking, and he's still a brilliant, if erratic young player. But how long will Tom Finn, his manager, coach and surrogate dad—

TOM: Christ, I'm sick of that!

FLICK: '… let the boy play up? Till he ends up on the scrap-heap of tennis history?'

STEPHANIE *and* JOSH *come in from the deck.*

STEPHANIE: Hi, Tom. You're back early.

*She looks at the table.*

You said lobster. What's this shit?

JASON *comes out of the kitchen with a jar of yeast.* JOSH *sees him and is dumbfounded.*

JASON: Don't touch those, please. They're laid out in order.

JOSH: Holy shit. Holy shit. Holy shit.

TOM: Stephanie, I think you're friend wants to be introduced.

STEPHANIE: Oh. Right. Jason, this is… [*to* JOSH] What's your name again?

JOSH: [*laughing heartily*] She's such a cut-up. Josh Makepeace.

STEPHANIE: Yes. Joss Makepeach.

FLICK: Steph, come and give me a hand in the kitchen.

JOSH: Oh, God, this is… awesome. Jason Strutt.

FLICK *hears this as she firmly steers* STEPHANIE *out.*

TOM: You're a tennis fan, Joss?

JOSH: Josh. I'm a Jason Strutt fan.

JASON: Thank you.

TOM: I thought you'd support one of your own boys.

JOSH: This guy is poetry. [*To* JASON] I saw you at Flushing Meadows. I felt like I was part of history.

JASON: History? Did you read this?

*He passes the* Herald *article.*

You have to do something, Finno.

TOM: Jason, I won't take on Vin Barnett. He's covering Tokyo. And he's right about Monte Carlo.

JOSH: [*still reading*] That was a bad line-call.

JASON: Thank you.

TOM: Bullshit. And he's reflecting public opinion.

JASON: That's not public opinion. This guy is public opinion.

JOSH: [*throwing down the* Herald] Where's his historical perspective?

They said this kind of thing about Mozart.

TOM: Mozart never threw his racket at the umpire's stand.

JASON: Do you know that for a fact?

TOM: No, but he probably never tossed a glass of guava juice over the front row of a press conference.

JASON: I bet he wanted to. I'd like to hear from his guy.

TOM: This guy... sorry, Josh, is it? Josh doesn't have to pick up the pieces after you.

JASON: I'd still like to hear from him.

JOSH: Well, I think you could modify his public profile.

TOM: I'd rather modify his turns on court.

JOSH: Like?

TOM: Like Monte Carlo.

JASON & JOSH: [*together*] That was a bad line-call!

JASON: [*to* JOSH] Thanks, Joss.

JOSH: Josh. As in Joshua. I fought the Battle of Jericho.

JASON: Yeah? When was that?

TOM: Josh, I'm not sure you should be encouraging Jason to think he's—

JOSH: Encouraging him to think. That's exactly what I'm doing. I say it's time he did some thinking for himself. And time you got some historical perspective.

JASON: Yes it is.

JOSH: Monte Carlo was an assertion of self. His identity was being questioned and he fought back.

TOM: A call went against him and he staged a tantrum. It's that simple.

JOSH: Simple? Mozart spent his first twenty years doing what Daddy wanted, Tom. Being a good boy. Playing by the rules. But he had to break out. And he gave the world *The Magic Flute*.

TOM: *The Magic Flute*? Well, Jason gave the world twenty-four hours of magic news photos, and I spent the next week mopping up. And that's not on. There's got to be some changes, Jason.

JASON: Says who?

TOM: Says me. Says Heidi.

JASON: Heidi doesn't know everything.

FLICK *and* STEPHANIE *enter with food.*

TOM: Heidi knows enough.

FLICK: Not enough to change the name.

JOSH: Look, Tom, nobody says to Mozart—

TOM: No more Mozart, okay?

JOSH: Okay, to Michelangelo, to Walt Whitman, make nice with the umpire. We're talking history, we're talking—

JASON: Poetry.

JOSH: Exactly. He's on the frontier, doing things the rest of us only dream about.

TOM: Like getting himself bucketed by every commentator on the circuit?

> JASON's *food is cleared off the table.* STEPHANIE *clears the yearbook and* Nyngan, *handing the latter to* JASON, *who looks at it.* STEPHANIE *starts to browse through the yearbook.*

JOSH: That's a failure of imagination. Sports stars are our present day avatars. In international competition, they purge the frustrations of contemporary society.

STEPHANIE: Is that what he was doing at Monte Carlo?

JASON & JOSH: [*together*] That was a bad line-call!

TOM: Bullshit.

JASON: Let's settle this right now.

FLICK: Let's eat!

> JASON *goes out of the room.*

STEPHANIE: Oh, will you look at these cheerleaders?

> FLICK *and* JOSH *exchange a glance of consternation.*

FLICK: Come and eat, Steph.

STEPHANIE: [*to* JOSH] And this is you! Winning the public speaking competition. Oh, Fliss, look at his hair!

TOM: That's your old school?

JOSH: Yes, I brought it in to show the girls.

> JOSH *holds out his hand.*

I guess I'll take it back now.

STEPHANIE: Not yet you won't. Get the hair!

> JASON *returns.*

JASON: Finno, what's happened to the Monte Carlo tape?

TOM: I don't much care tonight, Jason.

FLICK: [*trying to take the yearbook*] Steph, let's put this away. You're embarrassing your friend.

STEPHANIE: No man who's worn his hair like this can ever be embarrassed. Oh! Here's Fliss! You look so young! In the school play!

TOM: In the school play? In that book?

JASON: Here it is. In the VCR.

TOM: What's going on here?

>    JASON *starts the video.*

FLICK: [*on TV*] Look, what do you mean by fidelity? I think people can let one another down in lots of ways.

JASON: This isn't Monte Carlo.

FLICK: Turn it off.

>    JASON *does so.*

Thank you.

TOM: What's this school play, Flix?

JASON: Mrs Finn, I don't want to accuse you of anything, but did you wipe Monte Carlo?

TOM: I wiped it before I left. What was this play?

JASON: Why did you wipe it?

STEPHANIE: Can I see some more? It sounds wonderful. And I think the *Herald* sucks.

>    STEPHANIE *happily eats the lobster.*

TOM: What did they say, Flix?

FLICK: Nothing.

JASON: Why, Finno?

TOM: Shut up! What did they say?

FLICK: Nothing.

TOM: What did they say?

FLICK: [*suddenly very loud*] That I'm spiky and tense and surprisingly unsettled!

>    *There is a shocked silence.*

I can't think why.

TOM: Can I see the yearbook, please?

JOSH: No.

FLICK: [*handing it over*] Yes.

TOM: What is this?

FLICK: It's a churchyard. She's Lily. He's Amos. He's going off to war. It's an American national classic.

JASON: Finno, why did you wipe my tape?

TOM *looks at the yearbook.*

STEPHANIE: The lobster's fantastic, Fliss.

JASON: It's part of our archive, man. Where's your historical... what?

JOSH: Perspective.

JASON: Yeah, where is it?

TOM: [*absorbed in the book*] I'm working on it.

JASON: Mrs Finn, do you have any distilled water?

FLICK: No!

JASON: Boiled will do.

FLICK: Then go and boil some.

JASON: I can feel my system becoming totally unbalanced. That isn't good for Tokyo.

*He goes into the kitchen.*

TOM: Was it a good play?

FLICK: I thought so at the time.

TOM: Had you forgotten you were in it?

FLICK: I'd forgotten most of the lines. Can we talk about this in private?

JOSH: No, let's talk it out here.

FLICK: I'd like to be left alone with Tom!

*There is a knock on the door.* FLICK *throws up her hands and moves towards it.*

Well, who could this be? Dougal and Jean-Luc? The Jehova's Witnesses?

*She opens it.* BUNTY *comes in.*

Bunty.

BUNTY: Mission accomplished.

*She looks around.* STEPHANIE *is eating at the table.* JOSH *and* TOM *are standing.* TOM *still has the yearbook.*

Tom! You're back! But you missed the last twilight. Still you've met Joshua, isn't that nice? And you've heard all about Felicity's torrid adolescence. They were like that.

*She crosses her fingers.*

FLICK: Mother—

BUNTY: All three of them. Felicity and Joshua and Holly.

TOM: Holly?

BUNTY: Joshua's wife.

TOM: His wife.

JOSH: Ex.

STEPHANIE: Wife? Oh, no. He's gay.

BUNTY: Stephanie, a little sensitivity, please. He's going back to Holly tomorrow.

> JOSH *opens his mouth to protest.*

Yes, you are, dear. And be strong. Whatever you're going through is just a little phase, and I hope tonight's sorted a few things out for you.

> BUNTY *sees* TOM *with the yearbook.*

She's gorgeous, isn't she, Tom? Holly, I mean. Laid low by food poisoning tonight, and what a pity. It's turning into quite a party.

> *She looks at* STEPHANIE *who is still eating the lobster.*

Stephanie dear, I hope you're going to leave some of that for the others. Felicity's never too lavish in the portion department as it is. I know she wins all those awards, but what for? A snow pea and a Julienne carrot in a wasteland of white porcelain.

FLICK: How are the boys, mother?

BUNTY: They're fine. It was just one of those little flatmates' tiffs. And it soon sorted itself out. Dougal ate an entire tin of Walnut Surprise. Now they've asked me to bring down the yearbook.

TOM: I'm still looking at it, Bunty.

BUNTY: Give it here, you wicked thing. We can't all be married to a cheerleader.

> JASON *comes out of the kitchen, holding his hand.*

JASON: I scalded my hand on the kettle!

BUNTY: Hello, Jason. What a cross little face. You looked just like that at Monte Carlo.

JASON & JOSH: [*together*] That was a bad line-call!

BUNTY: Nonsense, dear, it was sheer bad temper. All the girls at tennis thought so.

BUNTY *takes the yearbook from* TOM.

Thank you, Tom. Those boys are dying to see what you were like at seventeen, darling. We're going to dangle our feet off the jetty and look at the pictures. It's a lovely night out there. A moon on the water, and a whole extra hour for dreaming. Why don't you all go out and enjoy it?

*She waves and goes out the door.*

FLICK: Yes, why don't you? Why don't you all go away while I speak to my husband? Alone.

JASON: We have to talk first, Finno. You sneak back into the country—

TOM: I never sneak.

JASON: You walk out on a major dinner—

TOM: With your contract in my pocket.

JASON: You wipe a tape from my archive.

TOM: Because I watched it back and I was disgusted. What do you want, Jason?

JASON: A want a bit of historical… what?

JOSH: Perspective. This is great, Jason. You're thinking for yourself.

*He goes into the kitchen.*

JASON: Yeah. I mean, look at the way they treated Mozart. And he never won at Wimbledon.

TOM: I don't want to hear any more about Mozart. Or you. I want to talk to my wife.

JASON: Heidi said you and me need to talk.

FLICK: There's that name again.

TOM: Later.

JASON: So we're going to talk.

TOM: Not tonight!

JASON: Oh, Tommy. I'm hurting inside. You know the pain, man. Nobody else understands. I'm really down.

*JOSH returns with whisky.*

And I've been down since Monte Carlo.

TOM & JOSH: [*together*] Well, that was a bad—

TOM: [*silencing* JOSH *with a look*] That was a bad mistake, mate.

*JASON begins to gasp slightly.*

JASON: But when you're out there on your own, it gets really tough…

JOSH: Are you okay?

JASON: It's alright, I'm just deeply depressed.

TOM: Calm down, Jase.

JOSH: You want some whisky?

TOM: Jason doesn't drink.

JASON: Just a glass of water. Boiled.

TOM: Sure. Flix?

FLICK: No.

TOM: The boy's upset.

FLICK: And the rest of us are just fine.

TOM: Well, the high school reunion seemed to be in full swing when I walked in—

FLICK: You didn't walk in. You were let in. Without your keys—

TOM: Yes.

FLICK: And your reading glasses. Straight from Heidi's poolside. Does she have a hot tub as well?

JASON: She has a rainwater tank.

FLICK: Shut up!

JASON: Do you have a rainwater tank?

TOM: Shut up!

JASON: Mineral water?

FLICK: Go home, Jason!

JASON: Give me a break, I only want—

FLICK: You only want. Exactly.

TOM: Leave the kid alone.

FLICK: The kid. The kid. What about this kid?

TOM: Oh, great. You get angry, you get righteous. You're the one who's had a dirty weekend.

STEPHANIE: With Jason?

JASON: With me? She's old enough to be my—

FLICK: Finish that sentence and you'll never live to see Wimbledon again.

JOSH: Jason, Stephanie, would you give us a bit of space here?

TOM: Us? Us! What's the story, Flix? Come on.

FLICK: Oh, Tom, don't play the disappointed coach. Nothing happened. But, oh, I was looking forward to it.

TOM: To what?

FLICK: To spending an evening with—

TOM: A night.

FLICK: Yes, all right, a night. A night with someone who didn't have to phone Dallas or take Jason to the naturopath. This was my night.

JOSH: Our night.

FLICK: You shut up, too. This was my night, Tom. No-one was supposed to be here. Not Bunty. Not Steph. Not the White City Amadeus. Just me and my old flame. I'm sorry I lied, but I'm sorrier that I had to. And I'm sorriest I didn't have any of it. Not the dinner, not the dancing, not the moon on the water. Nothing.

*She goes out the front door in distress.* JOSH *starts to follow her.* TOM *stands in his way.*

TOM: No way.

JOSH: See? She's thinking for herself too. Flicka!

*He makes for the door.*

STEPHANIE: [*stepping between them*] What do either of you care? Men are such bastards. Fliss?

*She runs out after* FLICK.

TOM: Oh, Christ. Flix?

*He too pursues* FLICK *out the door.*

Jason, I'll call you tomorrow.

JASON: Where's my water?

TOM: I haven't got time.

JOSH: [*offering the whisky bottle*] Take a hit of scotch.

TOM: Jason doesn't drink.

JASON: [*grabbing it*] What do you care?

JOSH: Right on, Jason. Personal liberation. [*To* TOM] You know something, pal? You don't deserve Jason Strutt—

TOM: You might be right there. Give it to me, Jason.

JOSH: Like you don't deserve Flicka. Because you don't understand them!

JASON: Yeah! What was that battle you fought in?

JOSH: You know why I'm here tonight?

TOM: I've made a fair guess.

JOSH: Same reason he's here. Personal liberation. This is the twilight of empire. Drink it, Jason, if that's what you want.

JASON *picks up a glass.*

TOM: No! Give it here, Jason.

*Turning, he sees that* JOSH *has slipped out the door.*

Oh, Christ! Put it down and go home, Jason. I can't let you do this to yourself.

JASON: You drink enough of it.

TOM: I'm not playing a six-figure tournament in Tokyo on Wednesday.

JASON: [*pouring a glass*] Maybe I'm not either.

TOM: You owe me better than this, son.

JASON: And what do you owe me? I've given you the best seven years of my life, and you've given me nothing but criticism and negativity. And now you're wiping my archive! I want some historical prospective.

TOM: Per.

JASON: What?

TOM: Perspective. And that's not what you want, baby, you want blood.

JASON: I want respect. I want you to stop them calling me names. 'The Killer from Kiama.' 'The Bad Boy from the Blow-hole'. I know why they do it.

TOM: Do you?

JASON: I can think for myself. I'm not stupid.

TOM: No. You're a very cluey young man. Jase, I don't know what to do with you.

JASON: Do with me? You don't own me. You didn't make me.

TOM: No. We made you together. And I don't like the job we did of it.

JASON: What do you mean? Don't you like me anymore?

TOM: I mean we've taken a wrong turning somewhere. And a lot of the fault is mine. Heidi's right, Jase. I think my life needs to change direction.

JASON: Yeah? Well, I think that battle guy was right. You don't deserve me.

TOM: Seven years says I do, Jase.

JASON: I know some other people who'd be very keen to handle this career. Maybe they can give me the right public profile.

TOM: Aren't you a bit young for plastic surgery?

JASON: Don't push me any further. Heidi told me to be ready to make some big changes.

TOM: Ditto.

JASON: You don't want to make me do anything rash, do you?

TOM: You've been doing fine on your own lately.

JASON: You're pushing me, Tom. I don't want to do it, but if—

TOM: Do what?

JASON: Sack you. If I had to sack you—

TOM: Sack me! You can't sack me, you... well, I suppose you can. Yes, you can, Jason. And you should. Big changes. Sack me.

JASON: What?

TOM: You know what we say, Jase. Find a strategy and stick with it. Come on. The golden handshake. The boot. The big A.

JASON: You can't do this to me

TOM: I'm not even asking for a reference.

JASON: What is this? It's your life.

TOM: No. Maybe it was once. Now it's airports and jet lag, and homicidal photographers with guava juice dripping off their lens caps.

JASON: What about the game? What about the buzz?

TOM: I can get all that on TV.

JASON: All right. All right. All right. One last chance.

TOM: Please, no.

JASON: You can't walk out on me like this.

TOM: Just watch me.

> TOM *makes for the door.*

JASON: Finno? I'm scared. Really scared.

TOM: No need to be, Jase. You're dynamite.

> *He offers his hand.* JASON *shakes it.*

Thank you.

JASON: Oh. You're welcome.

> TOM *goes out the front door.* JASON *goes to the telephone and dials an STD number.*

Hello?... Yes it's me... No, I'm not, I'm... I'm deeply depressed... Look, can I drive down and see you?... Tonight... why not tonight, I can be there in... Yes, I do, I do love you... thanks, Mum.

> JASON *hangs up. He packs his food containers, collects the* Herald, *and is going out when he remembers something else. He finds* Nyngan The Naughty Platypus, *stows it in his bag and hurries out, as the lights fade.*

*SCENE TWO*

JOSH *comes in via the deck. He has his shoes and socks in his hand, and his trousers rolled up. He looks round.*

JOSH: Flick?

> STEPHANIE *follows him in. She also has her shoes off. She carries a large sprig of frangipanni.*

STEPHANIE: Not here either?

JOSH: No. I was sure she'd be down by the water.

STEPHANIE: And I know what she must be going through. She's incredibly sensitive. We're very alike. We both internalise all our stresses, and just present this incredibly together front. But underneath... give me those lines again, will you?

JOSH: Walt Whitman?

STEPHANIE: Yes, I need them to pass on to... to a man I used to know.

JOSH: [*reciting*]

> I think I could turn and live with animals,
> They are so placid and self-contained,
> I stand and look at them long and long,
> They do not sweat and whine about their condition,
> They do not lie awake in the dark...

> STEPHANIE *mutters along with* JOSH.

STEPHANIE: 'And weep for their sins...' Fantastic. I'm just going to make a quick... private phone call.

> *She goes into the kitchen.* JOSH *pours a glass of whiskey. Someone is heard approaching via the deck.* TOM *enters. They look at one another in silence.*

JOSH: Where's Jason?

TOM: Gone home to finish *The Magic Flute*. Where's Flix?

JOSH: Flicka? Who knows. Out there by some stretch of water, I guess.

TOM: You were at high school together?

JOSH: Yep. And if it hadn't been for that goddam yearbook—

TOM: I had my doubts before.

JOSH: Yeah?

TOM: When she served me dinner. She'd never try and make one lobster stretch to three. Hadn't you better be going?

JOSH: Not till I see Flicka.

TOM: I think tonight's over, mate.

JOSH: Not according to your watch. You're still on Californa time.

TOM: That can be easily adjusted.

JOSH: You still don't have your latchkey.

TOM: Hey, what is this? The Gunfight at the O.K. Corral?

JOSH: The O.K. Corral. That's what Flicka used to call our school choir.

TOM: What?

JOSH: The Okay Chorale. But we were better than okay. We sang for all the right causes. The grape pickers, the Chicago Seven fighting fund... we liked a good challenge.

TOM: I can see that.

JOSH: And of course, we liked to sing.

*He starts singing lustily.*

   Shall we gather at the river—

TOM: Jesus!

JOSH: [*singing*] The beautiful, the beautiful, the river—

TOM: Look, mate—

JOSH: Shall we gather at the river—

TOM: Why don't you gather yourself into a car and piss off?

JOSH: You're getting hostile.

TOM: I'm getting things back into historical perspective.

JOSH: Meaning?

TOM: Meaning piss off.

   FLICK *enters from the deck.*

FLICK: What was that singing?

JOSH & TOM: [*together*] I've been looking for you.

*They stop and look at one another.*

   All night.

FLICK: The Okay Chorale.

TOM: We've already done that joke. How long has this reunion been planned?

FLICK: Nothing was planned. He rang the restaurant at lunchtime.

TOM: And flew in for dinner?

JOSH: Bad line-call.

FLICK: He was here to give a lecture. We haven't seen one another in twenty years!

TOM: Yet he knew where to find you.

FLICK: He saw me in a bar...

TOM: What!

FLICK: I mean, on TV in a bar, with Becker and Lendl.

TOM: So, he came for dinner.

JOSH: He? The name is Joshua Makepeace.

TOM: Makepeace? Bit wide of the mark.

FLICK: And he's flying out tomorrow night.

JOSH: Not necessarily.

FLICK: What? What do you mean?

JOSH: Later.

TOM: Later. There isn't going to be any later.

JOSH: Okay, here and now. My plans are flexible.

TOM: It must be the jet-lag. I could swear I heard you doing a line for my wife.

JOSH: I'm just talking travel plans.

TOM: All right. Piss off.

JOSH: Hey—

TOM: That's a travel plan.

JOSH: I could think of others.

TOM: Like what?

JOSH: Like coming back to the hotel with me.

TOM: Tonight? I'm sorry, I have a headache.

JOSH: Is that what you call playing the net? [to FLICK] The guy's into power, Flicka.

FLICK: The guy? His name is Tom Finn.

JOSH: The hot-shot manager. After he drove you out of the house tonight—

FLICK: He didn't drive me out, Josh. I went for a walk!

JOSH: And he stayed to lay this power trip on Jason. He can't let go, Flicka. [To TOM] Can you?

TOM: Let go of Jason? Well, it would be hard for me. Specially after all that's happened tonight.

JOSH: Are you hearing this?

FLICK: Go easy, Josh.

TOM: Forget the easy. Just go.

JOSH: Don't get territorial. You couldn't even remember your anniversary.

TOM: Oh, shit. Sorry. But I made it home.

JOSH: Without his latchkey.

TOM: Now that is a bad line-call. I got here, Flix. And before the clocks went back.

> STEPHANIE *comes serenely out of the kitchen, still holding the frangipanni.*

STEPHANIE: Oh, you're back, Fliss. We looked everywhere. I've just rung Brendan and given him up.

FLICK: At four o'clock in the morning?

STEPHANIE: Josh gave me the courage. And the words. 'Animals do not sweat and whine about their condition, they do not lie awake in the dark and weep for their sins.' Isn't that beautiful? Paul Whiteman.

TOM: [*to* FLICK] You organised this dinner-party, you wrap it up. And soon, please.

> *He goes into the kitchen.* STEPHANIE *touches* JOSH *with the frangipanni.*

STEPHANIE: He's wonderful, Fliss. So profound. What a waste. I'm going to sit on my deck and look at the moon on the water.

> *She wafts the frangipanni by them.*

Isn't this heaven? Something to dream on. Thanks for dinner, Fliss.

> *She goes off via the deck.*

FLICK: You were going home tomorrow.

JOSH: That can change.

FLICK: What about your classes? What about *Sacco and Vanzetti*?

JOSH: They'll live. I want to be with you.

FLICK: It doesn't worry you that my husband's in the next room?

JOSH: If it doesn't worry you. But we can always go somewhere.

FLICK: Tonight?

JOSH: Tonight, tomorrow, whenever.

FLICK: Josh, you have a life in California.

JOSH: Sounds like he does, too. Complete with swimming pool and hot-tub.

FLICK: Would you lay off Tom?

JOSH: Why? He doesn't deserve you.

FLICK: We have a marriage, Josh.

JOSH: Sure. You're married to him, he's married to Jason Strutt.

FLICK: Well, I'm sure you can relate to that.

JOSH: You heard him. He can't let go.

FLICK: That isn't quite what he said. And he has more to say.

JOSH: About this bimbo with the hot-tub?

FLICK: Maybe. But he did come back early.

JOSH: Without his latchkey.

FLICK: With something to say.

JOSH: And you can't figure it out what it is? Flicka, I do have a life in California. But it's very lonely. And tonight you tell me you're lonely too.

FLICK: True.

JOSH: This place is crazy. You need some personal space.

FLICK: True.

JOSH: And we had something special.

FLICK: True. That was a wonderful year. It was... something special.

JOSH: We could have that again. We could start over.

FLICK: You think so?

JOSH: I know so. We both felt it tonight. We have something.

FLICK: What I have, I don't know. What you have is a challenge. And you like challenges, Josh. Causes. Always did. Abbie Hoffman. Gene McCarthy. Holly.

JOSH: Holly?

FLICK: Yes. She must have been a challenge. A conquest. Am I right?

JOSH: What are you saying?

FLICK: I'm saying go home, Josh. It's very late.

JOSH: Not too late.

FLICK: Oh, yes.

JOSH: You'd let him back in? Without his keys?

FLICK: One thing at a time, Josh.

JOSH: Flicka, you can't just walk out on this!

FLICK: No, I can't. But you can.

> *She kisses him.*

Now go.

JOSH: 'If I go, I ain't going alone. I'm taking you with me, Lily.'

FLICK: Oh, Josh.

JOSH: 'The crocuses will bloom, and soon will come the harvest, and then the time for storing and setting indoors. But you'll go through all that time like a sleep-walker. For you'll be with me, wherever. You and this night, and this hush, and this moon.'

FLICK: That play… I thought it was so poetic…

JOSH: Yeah.

FLICK: And it's a crock of shit, isn't it?

JOSH: It's a national classic.

FLICK: Exactly.

JOSH: Goodbye.

*He kisses her.*

You're right.

FLICK: About what?

JOSH: Challenge. Conquest. I Was a Teenage Tamburlaine. Am. But tonight… that's not what I had in mind.

FLICK: You're sure?

JOSH: Back then, there was no conquest. No contest even.

FLICK: I was such a pushover?

JOSH: I was the pushover. You were a foreign powere. Foreign and surprising and funny. You still are. Thanks for dinner.

FLICK: My pleasure.

*He waves and goes out the door. After a moment she goes onto the deck and watches him on the road below. Suddenly she starts to laugh.* TOM *enters from the kitchen.*

TOM: He's gone?

FLICK: Yes.

TOM: For good?

FLICK: So to speak.

TOM: This is the first time?

FLICK: It would have been. And Heidi?

TOM: Heidi's done a lot for me.

FLICK: Great.

TOM: She sent me home a day early.

FLICK *looks at him, puzzled. He is smiling.*

I want to tell you about her.

FLICK: Don't do this to me, Tom. If you want to leave me, say so. But I can't bear all this smiling. Tell me. At least we'll be talking for once.

TOM: We always used to talk. Back then.

FLICK: Back then. I can scarcely remember what you were like, back then. Now, if you're here, you're busy, and if you're not... remember before we were married, you took me to hear that great woman... Sarah Vaughn. And she sang *The Nearness of You*? And we melted. These days it's a different song. The not-hereness of you.

TOM: Seemed to be okay by you tonight.

FLICK: For the first time in my life. And I would have kept quiet about it, I wouldn't have flaunted it like you.

TOM: Like me? Like how?

FLICK: 'Heidi sent me home a day early.' Really!

TOM: How do you see her?

FLICK: Like those girls in the yearbook. Big, blonde, nubile...

TOM: Nubile. She's seventy-eight years old. She has blue hair and fifteen cats. She's Jason's clairvoyant.

FLICK: Oh. This is the truth?

TOM: She's Jason's clairvoyant.

FLICK: And you couldn't have told me this before?

TOM: I was easing up to it. I didn't want you laughing.

FLICK: Why would I laugh? I know Jason has a clairvoyant.

TOM: But she's mine now as well.

FLICK: Your clairvoyant?

TOM: Don't laugh at me. She's infallible.

FLICK: Tom! Throw the I Ching, get your chart done, do any of that stuff, I don't mind, but don't tell me anyone's infallible.

TOM: She forecast Wimbledon.

FLICK: My mother forecast Wimbledon.

TOM: Jason swears by her. I thought she might be able to help sort him out.

FLICK: And?

TOM: She said come home tonight. And be prepared for some big changes.

FLICK: Oh, well! She's the new Nostradamus.

TOM: We're going to have a kid.

FLICK: According to Heidi?

TOM: According to me. If that's what you'd like.

FLICK: Oh, that's what I'd like. There's only one problem, Tom. We've already got one. So to speak.

TOM: No we haven't. Jason sacked me. Or I sacked him, I'm not quite sure which.

*Dawn begins to break.*

FLICK: But you said—

TOM: I said it would be hard to let him go. And it was.

FLICK: What will you do now?

TOM: Start something new. Just like Heidi said.

FLICK: Well, good old Heidi.

TOM: The chance of a child.

FLICK: She slipped you a fertility potion?

TOM: She drove me to the airport. I think we can manage the rest. She said, 'Cancel that dinner.' Just like you. She said, 'Go home before the clocks go back.'

*He kisses her. She is distracted.*

Was it sad saying goodbye to him?

FLICK: He was part of a good year. And I loved him. And tonight he made me remember what I was like. Yes, it was sad.

TOM: When I came out you were laughing.

FLICK: I watched him from the deck, going down to the road. He looked so forlorn. He walked to his car, stopped, looked up at the moon. Then he turned and sprinted up the steps to Stephanie's house.

*They start to laugh, quietly at first, then helplessly. Music is heard: Sarah Vaughn singing* The Nearness of You.

Hey, mister, can you stay a little longer?

TOM: Tonight I've got all the time in the world.

FLICK: Isn't that lucky? So have I.

*As the sun comes up, they begin to slowly dance together on the deck.*

## THE END

# www.currency.com.au

Visit Currency Press' website now to:

- Buy your books online
- Browse through our full list of titles, from plays to screenplays, books on theatre, film and music, and more
- Choose a play for your school or amateur performance group by cast size and gender
- Obtain information about performance rights
- Find out about theatre productions and other performing arts news across Australia
- For students, read our study guides
- For teachers, access syllabus and other relevant information
- Sign up for our email newsletter

**The performing arts publisher**

www.ingramcontent.com/pod-product-compliance
Lightning Source LLC
Chambersburg PA
CBHW041933090426
42744CB00017B/2045